MARBLE

EARTH'S ROCKS

Tracy Vonder Brink

NORWOOD HOUSE PRESS

Cataloging-in-Publication Data

Names: Vonder Brink, Tracy.
Title: Marble / Tracy Vonder Brink.
Description: Buffalo, NY : Norwood House Press, 2027. | Series: Earth's rocks | Includes glossary and index.
Identifiers: ISBN 9781978580114 (pbk.) | ISBN 9781978580121 (library bound) | ISBN 9781978580138 (ebook)
Subjects: LCSH: Metamorphic rocks--Juvenile literature. | Metamorphism (Geology)--Juvenile literature. | Rocks--Juvenile literature.
Classification: LCC QE475.A2 V66 2027 | DDC 552.4--dc23

Published in 2027 by
Norwood House Press
2544 Clinton Street
Buffalo, NY 14224

Designer: Rhea Magaro
Editor: Kim Thompson

Photo credits: Cover, p. 1 Parilov/Shutterstock.com; p. 3 R.M. Nunes/Shutterstock.com; p. 4 Kavic.C/Shutterstock.com; p. 5 Wikipedia; p. 6 Yes058 Montree Nanta/Shutterstock.com; p. 6 Krzysztof Bubel/Shutterstock.com; p. 7 Smelenna/Shutterstock.com; p. 9 BlueRingMedia/Shutterstock.com; p. 10 papa papong/Shutterstock.com; p. 11 Sanit Fuangnakhon/Shutterstock.com; p. 12 LUC KOHNEN/Shutterstock.com; p. 13 mlwebster/Shutterstock.com; p. 15 barbajones/Shutterstock.com; p. 16 Mehmet KILIC/Shutterstock.com; p. 18 lazyllama/Shutterstock.com; p. 19 New Africa/Shutterstock.com; p. 21 AofLine/Shutterstock.com;

Printed in the United States of America

CPSIA compliance information: Batch #CSNHP27: For further information contact Norwood House Press at 1-800-237-9932.

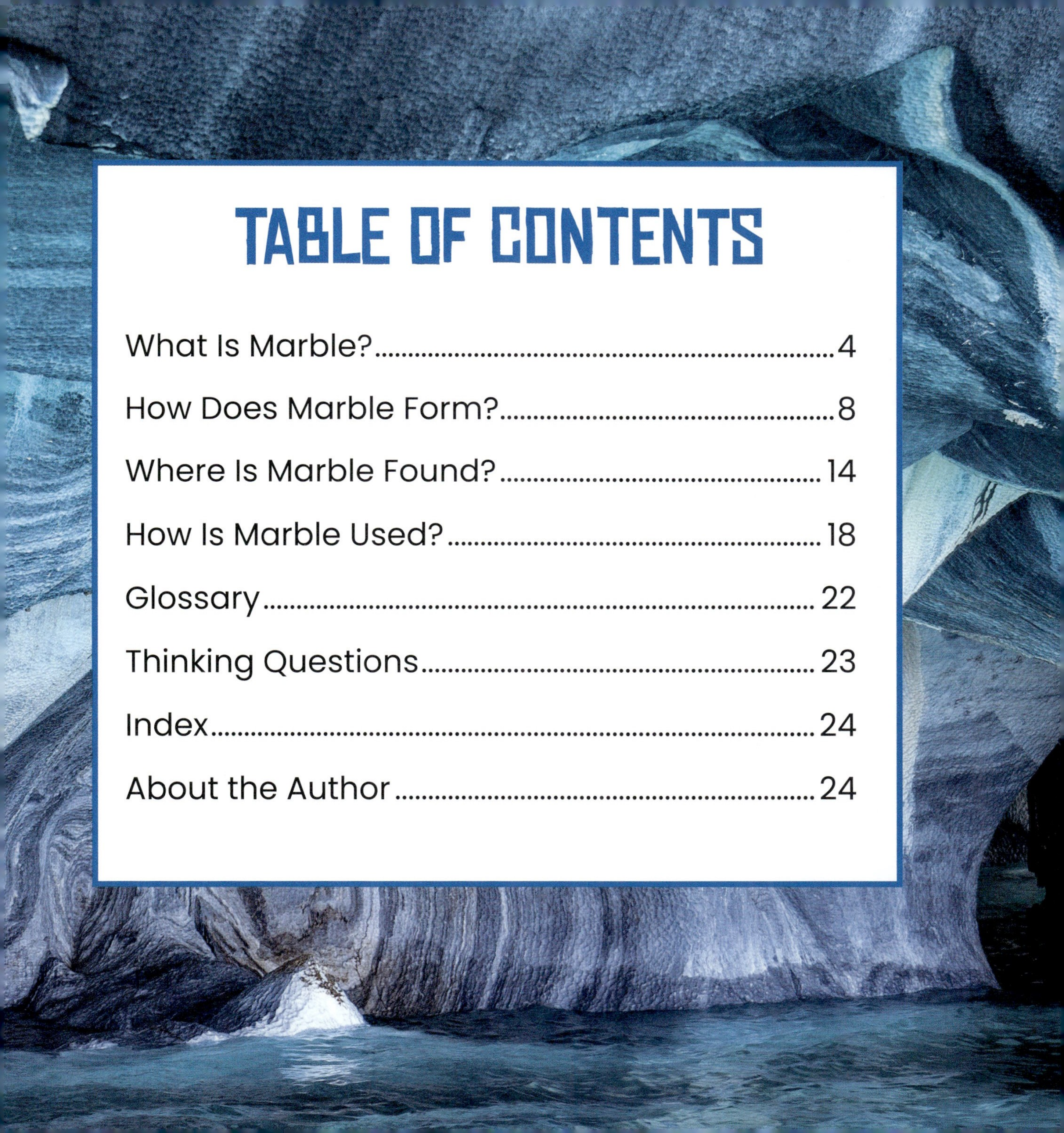

TABLE OF CONTENTS

WHAT IS MARBLE?

Rocks make up many things in the world, from tall mountains to the deep seafloor. All rocks are made of **minerals**. They are put into three main groups based on how they form.

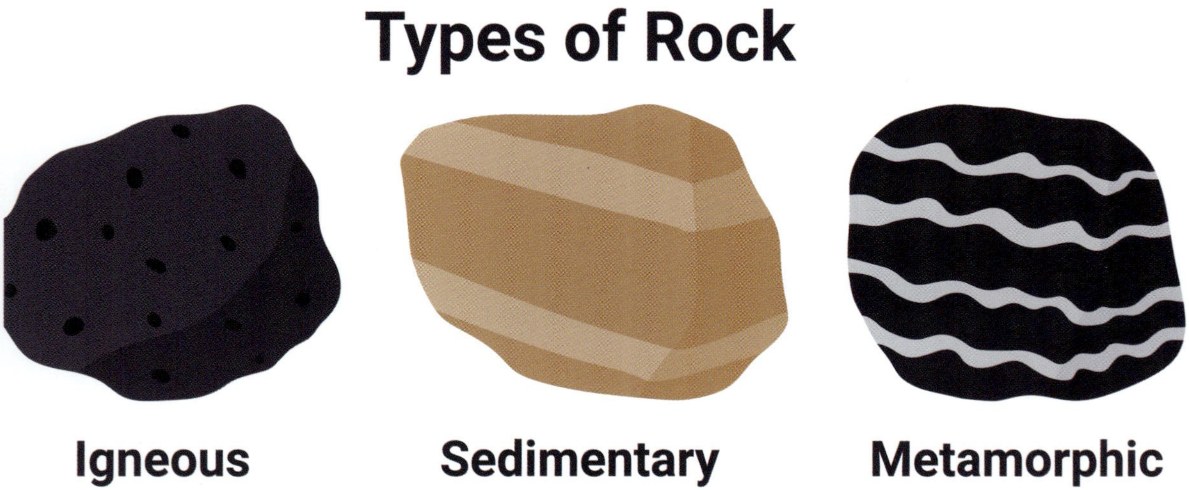

Metamorphic rocks start out as other rocks. The original rocks go through a **metamorphosis**. They change into a new kind of rock. Marble is a metamorphic rock.

Most marble forms from a sedimentary rock called limestone. Heat and **pressure** below Earth's surface change limestone into marble.

Marble is often light in color. It may be gray, green, yellow, or even pink. Some is pure white. White marble may have **streaks** of black.

HOW DOES MARBLE FORM?

Like all rocks, marble forms during Earth's rock cycle.

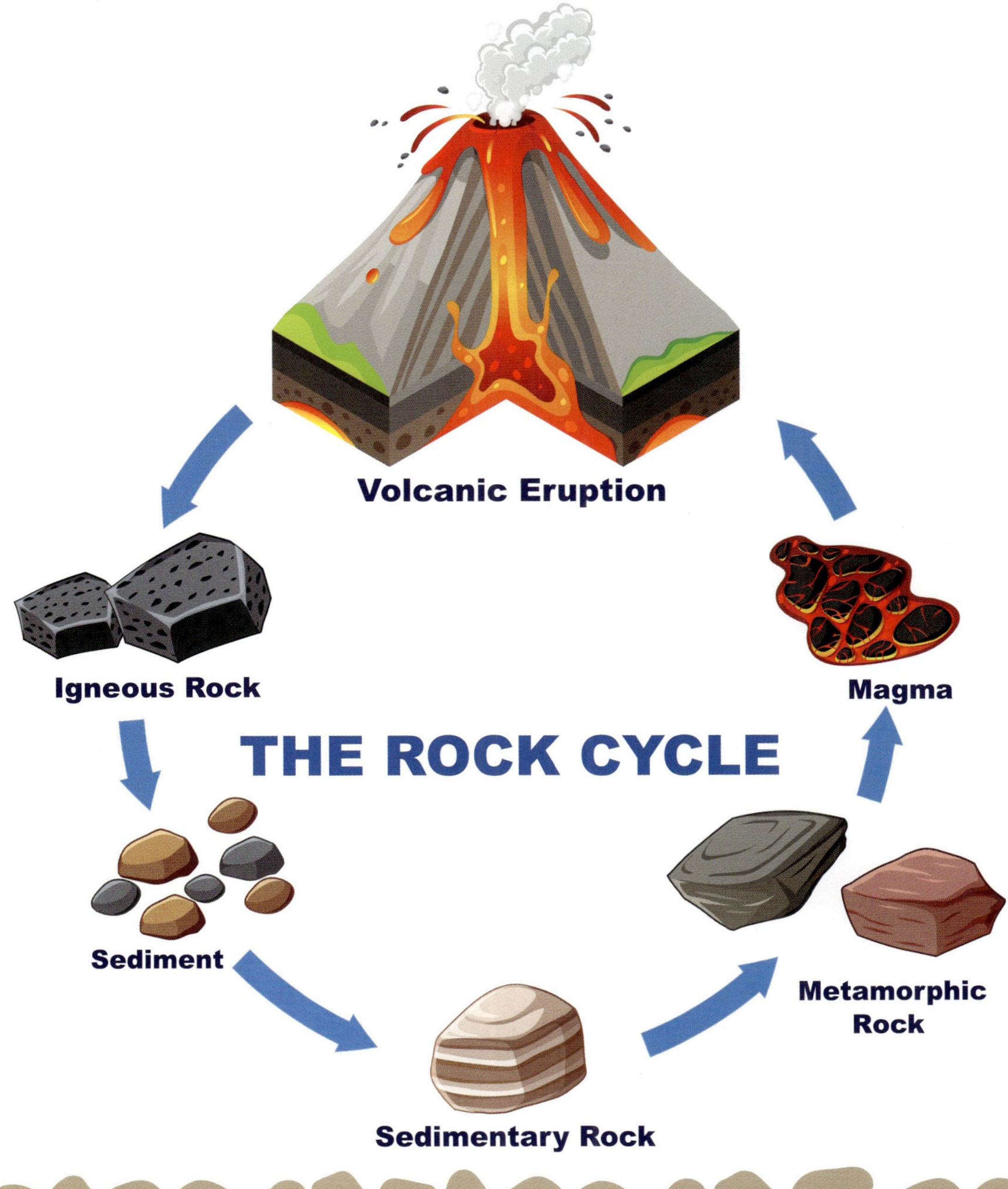
Volcanic Eruption
Igneous Rock
Magma
THE ROCK CYCLE
Sediment
Metamorphic Rock
Sedimentary Rock

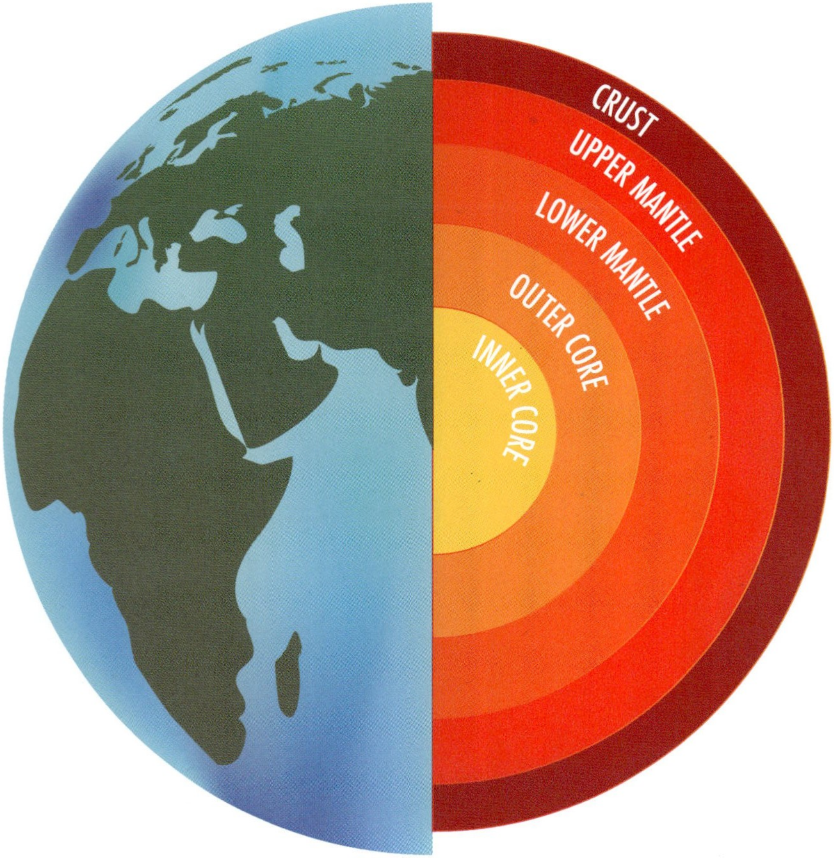

Earth has layers. The crust is the top layer. The mantle lies below. It's so hot in the mantle that rock melts into **magma**.

The crust is made up of huge pieces called **tectonic plates**. They move, even though we don't usually feel it.

Sometimes, plates run into each other. They push together so hard that they create lots of pressure. The pressure can shove rocks deeper into Earth's crust.

Sometimes, limestone gets pushed deep into Earth's crust. The pressure squashes the rock's minerals. High temperatures inside the crust heat up the rock. Heat also comes from magma that rises into the crust from the mantle.

Pressure and heat change the rock's minerals. The rock is no longer limestone. It becomes marble.

WHERE IS MARBLE FOUND?

Marble is found in and around mountains all over the world. Italy, China, Spain, and India **quarry** much of the world's marble. It's also produced in the United States, Greece, and Portugal.

Chile's Marble Caves are famous for their beauty. Lake water carved them out of marble cliffs over thousands of years. Visitors can tour the caves by boat.

HOW IS MARBLE USED?

People have used marble for thousands of years. Ancient Egyptians, Romans, and Greeks all used it to make statues and buildings. The Lincoln Memorial in Washington, D.C., is made from marble.

Marble can be crushed and mixed into concrete to make roads and sidewalks. Marble **slabs** are used as kitchen countertops. The minerals in marble are even in medicines for an upset stomach!

Marble is strong and beautiful. It is prized around the world for buildings that will stand the test of time.

GLOSSARY

magma (MAG-muh): melted rock below Earth's surface

metamorphosis (met-uh-MOR-fuh-sis): a complete or great change in appearance or form; a transformation

minerals (MIN-ur-uhlz): solids that form naturally in Earth and that do not come from an animal or plant; marble contains minerals such as calcite and quartz

pressure (PRESH-ur): the weight or force of something pushing on something else

quarry (KWOR-ee): to dig marble, slate, or other stones out of the ground

slabs (slabz): broad, flat, thick pieces of a material

streaks (streeks): long, thin marks or stripes

tectonic plates (tek-TAHN-ik playts): gigantic pieces of Earth's crust that fit together like puzzle pieces and that form continents and ocean floors

THINKING QUESTIONS

1. How are rocks put into groups?
2. What rock does most marble come from?
3. What might create the heat that makes marble?
4. Where is marble found?
5. Describe some of the ways people use marble.

INDEX

ABOUT THE AUTHOR

Tracy Vonder Brink is always curious about the world around her. She loves to make facts and true stories fun and has written many books for kids. Tracy lives near Cincinnati, Ohio, and enjoys reading, hiking, and playing with her two rescue dogs.